SNAPSHOTS IN HISTORY

SEPTEMBER 11

Attack on America

by Andrew Langley

SEPTEMBER 11

Attack on America

by Andrew Langley

Content Adviser: Derek Shouba, Adjunct History Professor
and Assistant Provost, Roosevelt University

Reading Adviser: Susan Kesselring, M.A., Literacy Educator,
Rosemount–Apple Valley–Eagan (Minnesota) School District

COMPASS POINT BOOKS
MINNEAPOLIS, MINNESOTA

COMPASS POINT BOOKS

3109 West 50th Street, #115
Minneapolis, MN 55410

Visit Compass Point Books on the Internet at
www.compasspointbooks.com
or e-mail your request to
custserv@compasspointbooks.com

For Compass Point Books
Jennifer VanVoorst, Jaime Martens, XNR Productions, Inc.,
Catherine Neitge, Keith Griffin, and Carol Jones

Produced by White-Thomson Publishing Ltd.
Tel.: 0044 (0)1273 403990
210 High Street, Lewes BN7 2NH

For White-Thomson Publishing
Stephen White-Thomson, Brian Krumm, Amy Sparks, Tinstar Design
Ltd. *www.tinstar.co.uk*, Derek Shouba, Joselito F. Seldera, Bill Hurd,
and Timothy Griffin

Library of Congress Cataloging-in-Publication Data
Langley, Andrew.
    September 11: attack on America / by Andrew Langley.
        p. cm. — (Snapshots in history)
    Includes bibliographical references and index.
    ISBN-13: 978-0-7565-1620-8 (hardcover)
    ISBN-10: 0-7565-1620-X (hardcover)
    ISBN-13: 978-0-7565-1823-3 (paperback)
    ISBN-10: 0-7565-1823-7 (paperback)
    1. September 11 Terrorist Attacks, 2001—Juvenile literature. I. Title. II.
Series.
    HV6432.7.L37 2006
    973.931—dc22   2005027143

CONTENTS

Attack on America

1

September 11, 2001, began as just another Tuesday morning at Logan International Airport in Boston. A line of 81 passengers filed through the security checkpoint, ready to board American Airlines (AA) Flight 11 bound for Los Angeles. They passed metal detectors and X-ray machines, specially designed to find weapons and other dangerous objects in pockets or luggage. The supervisors found nothing suspicious.

Not far away at the same airport, another group of travelers was being cleared to board United Airlines (UA) Flight 175, also bound for Los Angeles. They too passed through the security checkpoint without any problems. Everything seemed normal, and the passengers boarded the aircraft.

Things were more dramatic at Dulles International Airport, outside of Washington, D.C. There, passengers were being checked through security for American Airlines (AA) Flight 77. Three of them, Khalid al Mihdar, Nawaf al Hazmi, and Majed Moqed, set off an alarm as they walked past the metal detector. Even so, after another check, supervisors allowed them to board the aircraft.

The towers of the World Trade Center were a key element of the New York City skyline.

A surveillance video showed two hijackers passing through airport security.

Meanwhile, at the airport at Newark, New Jersey, there were no alarms. Thirty-seven passengers checked in for United Airlines (UA)

Flight 93, and they went quietly through the security routine. The screeners saw nothing suspicious about the passengers.

By about 8:00 A.M., these four flights were being loaded with passengers and luggage and were preparing for takeoff. According to the schedule, three of the flights were heading for Los Angeles. The flight from Newark was going to San Francisco. None of them would get there.

Soon after AA Flight 11's takeoff, five hijackers stood up from their seats. They stabbed two flight attendants with knives that had not been detected by the security system at the airport. Some hijackers herded the passengers to the rear of the aircraft, while other hijackers burst into the cockpit and took over the controls.

The huge Boeing 767 changed course and turned south. Flight attendant Amy Sweeney called up the control office in Boston and began to give a report of the terrifying scene. At 8:44 A.M., she said:

> *Something is wrong. We are in a rapid descent. We are all over the place. We are flying very, very low. We are flying way too low. Oh my God we are way too low!*

Then the call ended suddenly. At 8:46 A.M., AA Flight 11 smashed into the North Tower of the World Trade Center in New York City. Everyone on board was killed instantly.

Manhattan's financial district was just getting busy, as it did this time every weekday morning. The soaring twin towers of the World Trade Center were already filling up with office workers. High up on the 107th floor of the North Tower, early diners

Smoke poured from the World Trade Center's North Tower after AA Flight 11 smashed into the building.

were finishing their breakfasts in the Windows on the World restaurant. On the 91st floor, Steve McIntyre was starting work at his desk in the Bureau of Shipping.

Suddenly there was a massive roaring explosion. Flying at 470 miles per hour (756 kilometers per hour), the Boeing 767 of AA Flight 11 had ripped into the top of the North Tower, between floors 93 and 99. It was still carrying 10,000 gallons (37,854 liters) of fuel. Within seconds, the fuel ignited, sending a giant fireball flashing across the floors and down the elevator shafts as far as floor 22. Thick black smoke filled the upper floors.

In the amazement of that first moment, Steve McIntyre noticed that nothing moved in his office. Even his computer was still working. But moments later came the aftershock of the impact, rocking the tower from top to bottom. Rushing out of his office, McIntyre saw the thick smoke billowing up from the stairwell below him. Should he escape that way, even if it meant heading into the fire?

There was no choice. One look showed him that the stairwell going upward was completely blocked by huge chunks of shattered wall. The Boeing 767 had sliced into the building, blocking all three stairwells and cutting off access to all the floors above him. Steve McIntyre was one of the fortunate ones. The 1,344 people above McIntyre were trapped, with no way of getting out. Many more had been killed instantly by the impact of the aircraft.

At that very moment, UA Flight 175 was also being taken over by hijackers who shouted that they had a bomb on board. The attackers again had hidden box cutter knives, and they stabbed both pilots to death. Peter Hanson, one of the passengers, managed to phone his father:

> *I think they've taken over the cockpit. An attendant has been stabbed—and someone else up front may have been killed. The plane is making strange moves.*

The hijackers took the plane on a new course heading for New York City. Hanson made another call to his father:

> *It's getting very bad on the plane. Passengers are throwing up and getting sick. The plane is making jerky movements. I think we are going down. I think they intend to go to Chicago or someplace and fly into a building. Don't worry, Dad. If it happens, it'll be very fast. My God. My God!*

UA Flight 175 hit the South Tower of the World Trade Center at 9:03 A.M. Everyone on board was killed instantly.

Many people in the South Tower had been watching the events next door in horror. At first, hundreds had been moved out of the tower for safety reasons, but most had been allowed to return.

UA Flight 175 crashed into the World Trade Center's South Tower just minutes after the North Tower had been hit.

15

Stanley Praimnath was at his desk on the 81st floor when he looked out the window. He saw the 767 screeching toward him across New York Harbor, right past the Statue of Liberty.

The plane slammed into the building between the 77th and 85th floors, just 130 feet (39 meters) from where Praimnath was sitting. Its fuel tanks burst open, creating a vast fireball. The explosion blasted aircraft parts, furniture, computers, and electric cables in all directions. The tower staggered under the shock, swaying back and forth.

Praimnath, trapped in his office by debris, yelled for help. Others outside tore down a wall and released him. Together they dashed to the stairwell, which was covered with running water from shattered pipes. Flames and black smoke filled the air, but miraculously this stairwell was not blocked by rubble. Praimnath and his colleagues began to make their way downward.

Meanwhile, hijackers had taken over AA Flight 77 from Dulles Airport. They had forced it off its proper course and were headed south, back toward Washington, D.C. This was the way to the White House, the official residence of the U.S. president, as well as to the Pentagon, in Arlington, Virginia, and the headquarters of the U.S. Defense Department.

Several people on the ground near the Pentagon saw the approaching jetliner, traveling much too low and much too fast. Afework Hagos was stuck in a traffic jam on Columbia Pike.

He heard a violent screaming noise and quickly got out of his car as the plane roared overhead. People were running away in panic. The aircraft was tilting its wings up and down as if trying to get balanced, and it was flying so low that it was knocking down the streetlights.

Emergency vehicles raced to the scene, as smoke clouds filled the air after AA Flight 77 crashed into the Pentagon.

17

At 9:37 A.M., the Boeing 757 plowed into the western side of the Pentagon. The nose broke up and the wings flew forward. Then came the explosion of the fuel, engulfing the whole scene in flames and black smoke.

All 64 passengers and crew members were killed instantly, as were 125 workers inside the Pentagon.

So far, every hijacking had gone according to plan for the terrorists. But the last one, UA Flight 93, turned out differently. The aircraft had left Newark, New Jersey, at 8:42 A.M.—later than scheduled. At 9:28, air traffic controllers heard an emergency call from the pilot. Then he shouted:

Hey, get out of here—get out of here!

As the hijackers took over the cockpit, at least two people were stabbed, while the rest were herded to the back. The 757 changed course for Washington, D.C. Possibly the hijackers intended to target the White House.

Several passengers phoned family, friends, or work colleagues on the ground. Mark Bingham called his mother and left a brief message:

This is Mark Bingham. I love you.

Todd Beamer described events to an operator on the ground:

We're going down, we're turning round. Oh, I don't know. Jesus, please help us.

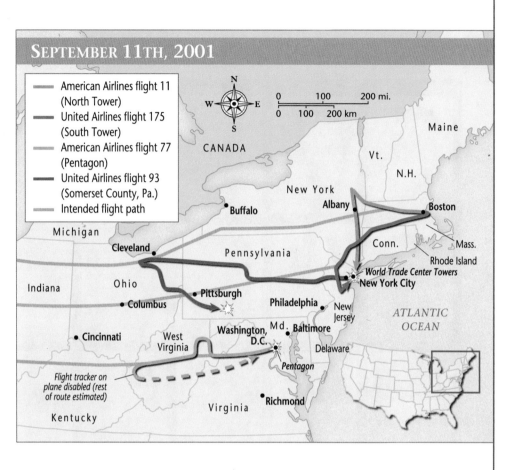

SEPTEMBER 11TH, 2001

- American Airlines flight 11 (North Tower)
- United Airlines flight 175 (South Tower)
- American Airlines flight 77 (Pentagon)
- United Airlines flight 93 (Somerset County, Pa.)
- Intended flight path

0   100   200 mi.
0   100   200 km

N W E S

CANADA

Maine

Vt.

N.H.

New York

Buffalo   Albany   Boston

Michigan

Cleveland   Pennsylvania   Conn.   Mass.

Rhode Island

World Trade Center Towers
New York City

Indiana   Ohio   Pittsburgh   Philadelphia   New Jersey   ATLANTIC OCEAN

Columbus

Cincinnati   West Virginia   Washington, D.C.   Md. Baltimore

Delaware

Pentagon

Flight tracker on plane disabled (rest of route estimated)

Kentucky   Virginia   Richmond

By speaking to people on the ground on their cell phones, they soon learned about the attacks on the World Trade Center. It was clear to them that they were all going to die, but there was one thing they could do first. They agreed to try to overpower the terrorists. At 9:57 A.M., Todd Beamer turned to the person sitting next to him and said:

The flight paths of the planes changed drastically after the hijackings.

You ready? Okay, let's roll!

Someone else shouted, "Let's get them!" Then air traffic controllers heard the sounds of a fight.

THE HIJACKERS

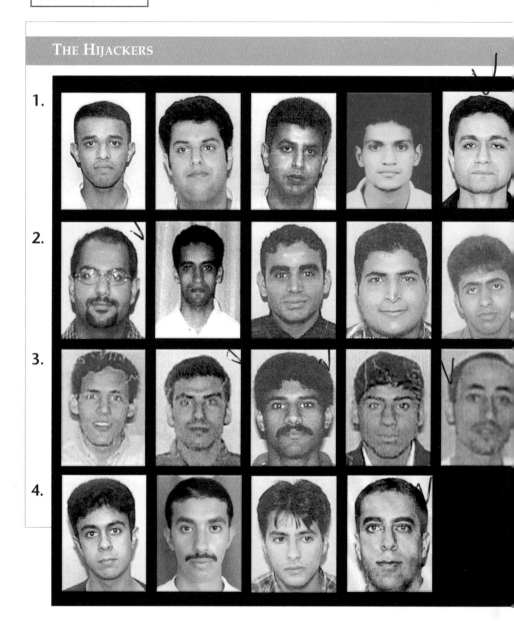

Ziad Jarrah, one of the terrorists, had taken over the aircraft's controls. He realized that he would soon be overpowered and put the plane into a dive.

The following men, pictured from left to right, are suspected of hijacking the four flights of September 11, 2001. Altogether, there were 19 hijackers on the four aircraft. Four were trained pilots, while the rest were responsible for keeping the passengers on the planes under control.

1. **American Airlines Flight 11** (Boeing 767—crashed into the North Tower of the World Trade Center) Satam al Suqami, Waleed al Shehri, Wail al Shehri, Abdulaziz al Omari, Mohammed Atta

2. **United Airlines Flight 175** (Boeing 767—crashed into the South Tower of the World Trade Center) Marwan al Shehhi, Ahmed al Ghamdi, Fayez Banihammad, Hamza al Ghamdi, Mohand al Shehri

3. **American Airlines Flight 77** (Boeing 757—crashed into the Pentagon) Majed Moqed, Khalid al Mihdhar, Nawaf al Hazmi, Salem al Hazmi, Hani Hanjour

4. **United Airlines Flight 93** (Boeing 757—crashed into a field in Shanksville, Pennslyvania) Saeed al Ghamdi, Ahmed al Haznawi, Ahmed al Nami, Ziad Jarrah

As it hurtled toward the ground, he shouted:

Allah is the greatest! Allah is the greatest!

UA Flight 93 plummeted into an empty field near Shanksville, Pennsylvania, at 10:03 A.M. Everyone on board was killed instantly. ◣

The Rise of Terrorism

The events of September 11, 2001, shocked the world. For the first time in history, terrorists had used airliners as guided missiles in a carefully planned attack on the U.S. mainland. They had killed about 3,000 people—mostly civilians—and toppled one of the most famous structures in the world.

The World Trade Center was a towering symbol of American pride and influence. The terrorists had shown that the most powerful nation on Earth was unable to protect itself against a handful of fanatical and determined men.

The atrocity of September 11 was carried out by extremist followers of the Islamic religion. But the September 11 attack was not a battle in an official war between nations, nor was it

aimed at defeating armies, conquering land, or gaining riches. Instead, it was part of a worldwide campaign of terrorism, aimed at causing fear, chaos, and death.

This campaign was being waged by dozens, perhaps hundreds, of different groups from many different countries. Some of them were acting on their own, while others were working together, guided by influential leaders. Many thought that the mastermind behind the attacks was a terrorist named Osama bin Laden. He had declared a struggle against the United States in 1998 in which he vowed to kill Americans and their allies.

The South Tower of the World Trade Center collapsed in a mountain of smoke and debris in about 10 seconds.

In the days and weeks after the bloody hijackings, ordinary people asked themselves bewildered questions. What was the purpose of the attacks? Why would anyone want to kill innocent people? Whom can we blame for the murders and humiliation? Why do these extremists hate the United States so much? How can we protect ourselves against more suicidal outrages?

The answers to these questions are not simple. Some lie in the recent history of relations between the United States and countries of the Middle East and Asia. Others are found much farther back in time, with the growth of three of the world's most widespread and popular religions—Judaism, Christianity, and Islam.

All of these religions are very old, and all of them began in the Middle East. Judaism, the faith of the Jewish people, evolved more than 3,000 years ago in the region now occupied by Israelis and Palestinians.

The same area saw the beginning of the Christian religion about 2,000 years ago. Islam was also founded in the Middle East, in the region now called Saudi Arabia, about 1,400 years ago.

In the centuries since, people of these three faiths have mostly lived side by side in peace. They have formed alliances, traded with each other, and exchanged ideas and knowledge. Of course, like all neighbors and rivals, they have sometimes fought one other. Some of their wars have been very savage indeed.

In about 1070, Muslim forces conquered the lands of Syria and Palestine, which included the city of Jerusalem and other places that were holy to Christians. This alarmed the leader of the Roman Catholic Church and many rulers in Europe, and in 1095 they sent armies to drive out the Muslims. So began the Crusades, a long series of bitter conflicts that lasted for nearly 200 years. During this period, thousands of people died, but the Christians never managed to permanently gain control of the region.

The Dome of the Rock in Jerusalem is one of Islam's holiest sites. Muslims believe that the prophet Mohammed ascended from there to receive commandments from God. The Church of the Holy Sepulcher, a site Christians consider sacred, is near the Dome.

Over the following centuries, Muslims and Christians both built up large empires, which stretched across the world from North America to Asia.

But, by about 1900, the Islamic world, led by the Ottoman Turks, had grown somewhat weak. While the Industrial Revolution had brought riches and power to the Christian countries of Europe and North America, the Muslim countries had lagged behind. Many Muslim countries had

also fallen into the hands of Western powers. The British ruled Egypt and the partly Muslim India, while the French ruled Algeria. During World War I (1914–1918), the armies of the Ottoman Empire fought on the losing side with Germany. After this shattering defeat, most of the land on and around the Arabian Peninsula was divided up among the victorious nations. Great Britain took over Iraq, Palestine, and other areas, while Lebanon and Syria were given to France.

During World War I (1914–1918), Turkish troops fought to keep control of the region then called Palestine.

27

Most people in this region were deeply troubled and humiliated by their new foreign rule. Not only were they being governed by foreigners, but those foreigners were non-Muslims. Many of the most sacred Islamic sites, such as the Al-Aqsa Mosque in Jerusalem and the holy mosque of Mecca in Saudi Arabia, were under the control of people who were infidels, or non-believers.

During the 1920s and 1930s, there were several rebellions against European rule, notably in Iraq and Syria. This period also saw the beginning of a dramatic new movement for reform in the Muslim world. We now call it Islamic fundamentalism. The first important fundamentalist group was the Muslim Brotherhood in Egypt. Its members believed that the new rulers of Egypt and several other countries of the Middle East were becoming less religious and were following the corrupt ideas of the Europeans and Americans, collectively known as the West. The Brotherhood vowed to take power in these traditional Muslim states and to bring back stricter Islamic values.

The Muslim Brotherhood was hugely popular and by 1945 had more than two million followers. This made them a threat to successive Egyptian governments, many of which wanted to make their country more modern and prosperous. The Egyptian rulers took savage measures to stamp out the Brotherhood during the 1950s. Even so, the fundamentalist movement kept growing. Many Muslims were unhappy with the increasing Western influence on their society.

This unhappiness turned to anger when the United Nations established the modern state of Israel in 1948. The aim was to provide the Jewish people with a homeland after the horrors they had suffered at the hands of the Germans in World War II.

Israeli soldiers built barricades in city streets to guard against attacking Egyptian, Iraqi, Syrian, and Palestinian troops after Israel was formed in May 1948.

Israel was created by splitting the historical territory of Palestine into two parts. Part of the territory became Israel, a homeland for the Jewish people, and the rest became a much smaller area for Palestinian people. The creation of Israel caused great bitterness among Muslims and Palestinians, who believed that their land was being stolen from them. It marked the beginning of a long conflict that has continued ever since.

One of the most important inspirations for Islamic fundamentalists was an Egyptian named Sayyid Qutb (sī'yid kŭ'tub).

ISLAM

The word Islam means "obedience" to Allah, the one true God. Followers of the Islamic faith are called Muslims. They follow the guidance of Allah in their daily lives, which are built upon the Five Pillars of Islam—believing in Allah, praying regularly, giving money to the poor and needy, fasting during the time of Ramadan, and making a pilgrimage to the Holy City of Mecca. Mecca was the birthplace of the Prophet Mohammed, who founded Islam. Muslims believe that Mohammed was the last true prophet, in a line that included Adam (the first human) and Jesus. Today there are at least 1.3 billion Muslims in the world.

An intense and very serious man, he wanted a return to the customs of old-fashioned Islam. The sight of women without veils in Cairo shocked him so deeply that he never married.

In 1948, Qutb traveled to study teaching methods in the United States. What he saw there made him even more horrified. The whole American way of life seemed to be corrupt and immoral, from loud jazz music in nightclubs to the empty and irreligious lives of most suburban homeowners. Qutb said:

> *Nobody goes to church as often as Americans do. Yet no one is as distant as they are from the spiritual aspects of religion.*

He felt that Western civilization was heading for disaster and that the only way to save the Islamic world from a similar fate was to revive the power of Islam. Qutb thought that all Muslims should join together in a *jihad*, or struggle, against the tyranny of non-believers.

Back in Egypt, Qutb became a militant, or a person aggressively active in a cause. He wrote several important books. His ideas grew more violent and extreme, and he argued that the whole world should eventually be made to follow the Islamic faith. He wrote:

> *The peace of Islam means that all people should obey Allah alone, and every system that permits some people to rule over others be abolished.*

Qutb's views alarmed Egyptian government leaders. In 1965, he was arrested for plotting to overthrow the government. Government actions like this created some of the drive for the development of Islamic fundamentalism.

Crisis in Afghanistan

The teachings of Sayyid Qutb lived on, and the events of the next 20 years seemed to give them extra force. First came the war between Israel and neighboring Arab states in 1967. This war lasted only six days, but in that time, Israeli armies invaded parts of the territories of Egypt, Jordan, and Syria. An Arab attempt to win back this land in 1973 did not succeed. It was a fresh humiliation, and many Muslims were enraged to see that Israel was being supported by the U.S. government.

During the 1970s, however, several Middle Eastern countries showed that they had a new kind of power—economic power. This power came from oil, the most important fuel in the world. Saudi Arabia and its neighbors controlled the biggest supply of oil, which meant that they had a growing influence on the world economy. When the price of oil rose rapidly, increased riches began to flow into these Arab states, which had been poor only a short time before.

With this power came a growing confidence. In some countries, there was a revival of support for traditional Muslim ideals and values, encouraged by the teachings of men such as Qutb. This happened dramatically in Iran in 1979, where the shah (ruler) was overthrown in a popular uprising of Islamic fundamentalists headed by the Ayatollah Khomeini. His followers broke into the U.S. Embassy in Tehran, Iran, and took 66 American hostages.

Later that year, an even bigger crisis erupted. It was to have far-reaching effects on the future of the fundamentalist cause and would inspire the terrorist career of Osama bin Laden. In December, troops of the Soviet Union invaded the strongly Muslim country of Afghanistan. Soon they were in control of the main cities and had installed a communist government.

THE POWER OF OIL

In 1938 American surveyors discovered huge amounts of petroleum beneath the ground in Saudi Arabia, Iraq, and other nearby areas. This brought huge wealth to what had been a very poor part of the world. At first, the operation of the oil fields was in the hands of American companies such as Aramco in Saudi Arabia. But as world demand for oil skyrocketed in the 1970s, governments in these countries took control of their oil. Today, the Middle East is still the most important oil-producing area in the world, with more than 60 percent of the world's petroleum reserves.

However, outside the towns there was ferocious resistance to the invaders. Afghan fighters, joined by thousands of volunteers from all over the Islamic world, fought back against the Soviet forces. They used guerrilla tactics—ambushing patrols, making swift hit-and-run attacks, and shooting down enemy helicopters with rockets. The Soviets could not defeat them, even with their superior weapons.

During their war of resistance against the Soviet invasion, Afghan guerrillas often traveled on horseback because of the rough terrain.

34

The U.S. government secretly gave arms and support to the Afghan resistance movement. At this point, the United States was on the same side as many Muslim nations, who were also sending weapons and money to help oppose the Soviet invasion.

Osama bin Laden was among the hundreds of volunteers who came to Afghanistan to take part in the jihad against the Soviets. Using his family's wealth, he helped build training camps, and he shipped equipment to the guerrillas. He also proved himself to be a fearless fighter, taking part in many military operations against Soviet troops.

THE SOVIET UNION

At the end of World War II in 1945, there were two superpowers in the world—the United States and the Soviet Union. The Soviet Union was a huge federation of communist states that also ruled many of the nations of Eastern Europe. Its aim was to spread communism to the rest of the world. Conflict with the United States led to a Cold War, during which the countries threatened each other did not fight openly. Instead, wars were fought by smaller nations, under the control of one or the other of the superpowers. The Cold War ended with the breakup of the Soviet Union in 1991.

By early 1989, the Soviets had given up the bitter struggle and withdrawn their soldiers from Afghanistan. The Afghans and other Muslims rejoiced in their victory. At last, the forces of the Islamic nations had scored a decisive blow against an infidel nation that had tried to conquer their territory. The triumph clearly showed that a loosely organized band of fanatical guerrillas could defeat a stronger, better-trained, and better-equipped enemy.

After fighting for about nine years, the last Soviet troops left Afghanistan in February 1989.

Abdallah Azzam, a powerful Palestinian preacher who had a huge influence on Osama bin Laden, wrote of the struggle:

> *This duty will not end with victory in Afghanistan. Jihad will remain an individual obligation until all other lands that were Muslim are returned to us, so that Islam will rule again.*

Azzam, like many other extremists, saw the defeat of the Soviets in Afghanistan as a massive triumph for the forces of Islam. He also saw far beyond this. Now that the Muslims had a guerrilla

HOW SOME MUSLIMS SEE THE UNITED STATES

Madonna and Michael Jackson are torchbearers of American society, with their cultural and social values. They are destroying humanity. They are ruining the lives of thousands of Muslims and leading them to destruction—away from their religion, ethics, and morality.

Paul R. Pillar, Pakistani scholar and writer

They violate our land and occupy it and steal the Muslim's possessions, and when faced by resistance they call it terrorism.

Osama bin Laden, terrorist leader

army and the finances and training to back it up, the message of Islamic fundamentalism could be carried to other parts of the world.

This was an ambitious idea, though it was also unrealistic. There were certainly many countries where Muslims needed help, but few of them had the same aims. Many Palestinians wanted to establish their own state, free from Israeli domination. Muslims in Bosnia wanted to be safe from attacks by Orthodox Christian Serbs. Fundamentalists in Algeria (already a Muslim country) had won a general election, but military and civilian chiefs prevented them from taking power. Muslims rebelled against their governments in places as far apart as the Philippines, Burma, Somalia, and Chechnya.

37

Each of these movements was different and separate. They were never part of a worldwide Islamic plot. Their leaders did not work together but tended to fight on their own and for their own reasons.

Several uprisings even saw Muslims fighting other Muslims. However, there was one thing that all these extremists agreed on: They hated the power and influence of the West. And the main focus of this hatred was the United States.

Fundamentalist Muslims saw the United States as a direct threat to the future of Islam. They believed that the United States promoted a non-religious way of life and was a corrupt and bullying society. Just as Sayyid Qutb had been horrified by loud dance music and the carefree behavior of Americans, later extremists were also disgusted by what they saw as the immoral behavior of people from the West.

On top of this, many people thought that the U.S. government was determined to impose its influence on other parts of the world. They thought that fast food consumption, flashy television advertising, an obsession with material goods (such as expensive tennis shoes and cars) and a greed for the Earth's resources were quickly spreading into other cultures.

The United States also seemed to many people to be building up a new empire (in Central America, for example) in the mid- and late 1900s. In addition, the U.S. government was accused of

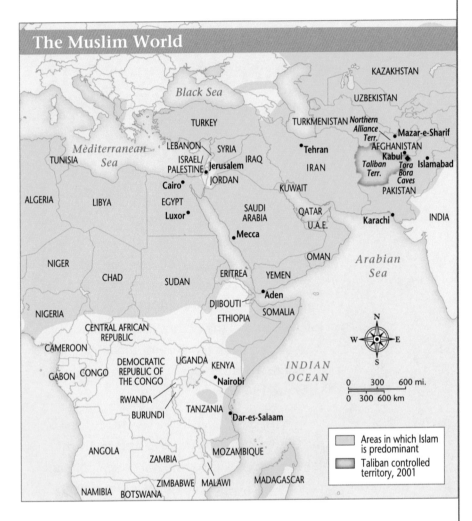

The Muslim World

KAZAKHSTAN

UZBEKISTAN

Black Sea

TURKEY

TURKMENISTAN Northern
Alliance
Terr. •Mazar-e-Sharif

AFGHANISTAN

Mèditerranean LEBANON SYRIA •Tehran Kabul•◆

TUNISIA *Sea* ISRAEL/ IRAQ IRAN Taliban Tora Islamabad
PALESTINE Jerusalem Terr. Bora
JORDAN Caves

Cairo• KUWAIT PAKISTAN

ALGERIA LIBYA EGYPT SAUDI QATAR Karachi• INDIA
Luxor• ARABIA U.A.E.

•Mecca

OMAN *Arabian*

NIGER *Sea*

CHAD ERITREA YEMEN
SUDAN •Aden

DJIBOUTI

NIGERIA ETHIOPIA SOMALIA

CENTRAL AFRICAN N
REPUBLIC

CAMEROON W E

DEMOCRATIC UGANDA KENYA *INDIAN* S
GABON CONGO REPUBLIC OF *OCEAN*
THE CONGO •Nairobi 0 300 600 mi.

RWANDA 0 300 600 km
BURUNDI TANZANIA
•Dar-es-Salaam

ANGOLA MOZAMBIQUE

ZAMBIA

ZIMBABWE MALAWI MADAGASCAR
NAMIBIA BOTSWANA

☐ Areas in which Islam
is predominant
☐ Taliban controlled
territory, 2001

forging links with authoritarian regimes, such as
that in Egypt, where government leaders—not
the country's people—had final authority about
the way the country would be run. U.S. leaders also
had the weapons and the money to support their
ideas and projects. It was easy for many Muslims to
believe that the West was anti-Islamic. ◀

*The map shows
areas of Africa in
the Middle East
in which Islam
is predominant,
and the area of
Afghanistan which
were controlled by
the Taliban in 2001.*

First Strikes on the West and Its Allies

4

An Islamic revival had began in the 1970s that had been an idealistic and largely peaceful movement. However, by the late 1980s, the movement was turning into what many people thought to be an ugly and violent campaign of murder. People like Abdallah Azzam urged Muslim fundamentalists to declare a universal war against the United States and its allies.

For this, they needed a devoted terrorist army and a base for training and instruction. Afghanistan, engulfed in war since the late 1970s, was the perfect hideout. Its neighbor, Pakistan, was also a refuge for many militant Muslims. From about 1989, these countries became the nursery of a new, radical kind of Islam.

Hundreds of militants flocked to the training camps set up near the Afghanistan-Pakistan border by various fundamentalist groups. Few of these volunteers had any military training. After being taught the basics of how to fire rifles and heavier weapons, they had lessons in handling explosives and making bombs. Besides this practical work, they attended lectures on Islamic law and the vision of their global struggle. The best warriors were selected to carry out terrorist activities outside Afghanistan.

Militant leaders trained rebels about weapons and warfare at training camps in Afghanistan.

It was not long before this international campaign moved into action. The first strike against the United States took place on American soil. On February 26, 1993, a huge bomb exploded beneath the World Trade Center in New York City, a symbol of the commercial might of the United States. It was packed inside a van that had been left in an underground parking lot. Six people died and more than 1,000 were injured. The explosion caused damage to seven floors of the trade center.

THE TWIN TOWERS

When they were completed in 1971, the towers of the World Trade Center were the tallest buildings in New York City. Their 110 stories reached 1,352 feet (415 meters) into the sky. They were each constructed of vertical steel columns, held in place by horizontal steel trusses. Each tower had 99 elevators and three central stairwells running top to bottom. When the offices and other facilities in the towers were full, they could hold more than 50,000 people.

A Pakistani man named Ramzi Yousef had rented the van, constructed the bomb, and driven it to the World Trade Center. He had been in the United States for just six months, after a long period of training in the Islamic guerrilla camps of Pakistan. A few hours after the bomb went off, he flew back to Karachi, Pakistan, and disappeared. Ramzi was eventually arrested in Pakistan two years later and boasted at his trial that he had wanted to knock over one of the twin towers. However, he probably had no link with Osama bin Laden.

The militants also turned their fury on the governments of Muslim countries that they believed were not religious enough, or that were friendly toward the United States. In June 1995, Islamic terrorists tried to murder Hosni Mubarak, the president of Egypt. In November of that year, they detonated a large bomb that totally destroyed the Egyptian Embassy in Islamabad, Pakistan, killing 16 fellow Muslims.

Inspectors and police officials investigated the bombing of the Egyptian Embassy in Islamabad, Pakistan, in November 1995.

By 1996, fundamentalist terrorism was shaking the world and causing deaths among people of all faiths, including Islam. A truck-bomb blast in Saudi Arabia killed 19 Americans. In Algeria, the long war between the government and militants had already killed 50,000 people. In 1997, an Islamic group massacred 58 European vacationers near Luxor in Egypt,. Extremists in Pakistan drove hundreds of native Christians from their homes in that country's Punjab province.

Few of these atrocities were the work of Osama bin Laden, and his name was still little known. But early in 1998 he made his first entry into the world spotlight. At a press conference in Afghanistan, he announced that he was forming a World Islamic Front, which would carry on a struggle against the United States. Bin Laden said:

> *To kill Americans and their allies is an individual duty for every Muslim who can do it in any country in which it is possible to do it.*

Many were ready to obey the call to jihad. On August 7, 1998, two car bombs exploded within minutes of each other outside U.S. embassies in East Africa. The combined toll in Nairobi, Kenya, and Dar-es-Salaam, Tanzania, was 224 dead, almost all of whom were Kenyans.

There was a swift response to this outrage from U.S. leaders in Washington, D.C. Two weeks later, U.S. warships in the Persian Gulf launched Cruise and Tomahawk missiles to attack what they hoped were a bin Laden base in Sudan and a headquarters in northeast Afghanistan.

Terrorist bombs damaged the U.S. Embassy in Nairobi, Kenya, in August 1998.

Buildings were destroyed, and 23 were people killed, but bin Laden was not among the dead. Many experts believed that the armed forces had picked the wrong targets.

The missile strikes were intended to reassure Americans and send a stark warning to the terrorists. However, for many Muslims they had the opposite effect, turning Osama bin Laden into an Islamic fundamentalist hero who had stood up to the United States. Few Muslims had heard of him before, but now many saw him as a major figure. What is more, the strikes convinced many people that the U.S. government really was hostile to Islam.

OSAMA BIN LADEN

Osama bin Laden was born in 1957 in Saudi Arabia. He was the son of a millionaire builder. Shy and very serious, he studied engineering in Jeddah, Saudia Arabia. There, he came under the influence of the militant Islamist preacher Abdallah Azzam and also the brother of Sayyid Qutb. Bin Laden went to Pakistan in the early 1980s, where he helped recruit and train guerrilla fighters. By 1996, he had been expelled from Saudi Arabia because of his extreme views and the Sudan because of U.S. pressure. He took refuge in Afghanistan. After September 11 and the U.S. invasion of Afghanistan, he disappeared without a trace.

Militant Islam also had a triumph to boast about. In shattered Afghanistan, an extreme fundamentalist group called the Taliban came to ruling power in the mid-1990s. The Taliban imposed a strict and old-fashioned version of Islamic law on the Afghan people—one in which televisions were forbidden and men were not

Osama bin Laden spoke to reporters in 1998, the same year he declared that killing Americans was a duty of every Muslim.

allowed to trim their beards. The strictest rules applied to women. They could not go to school or take jobs and were forced to cover themselves from head to toe in long dark robes called *burkas*.

47

The Taliban was pleased to shelter Osama bin Laden and other militant leaders. Meanwhile, the training of terrorists continued in the camps of southern Afghanistan. Among those who learned their craft there were the men behind the next dramatic blow against the United States. On October 12th, 2000, a small boat filled with explosives rammed the American destroyer USS *Cole* near the harbor of Aden in Yemen. The blast ripped a hole in the ship's side, killing 17 crewmembers.

This time the Americans did not hit back with an air strike. But Osama bin Laden still gained publicity for his campaign. Immediately after the

After being the target of a terrorist attack, the USS Cole *was towed into open sea by a military tugboat on October 29, 2000. A bomb had ripped a hole (see arrow) in the port side of the ship.*

48

Cole attack, he produced a video showing his militant fighters in training and images of the *Cole* explosion. This was soon broadcast on television networks all over the world, including CNN and Al-Jazeera, an Arabic-language television network.

Even then, the next assault on the United States was being prepared. It was going to be more complex than anything that had been attempted before. It would also require an entirely new element—trained aircraft pilots. The pilots and other terrorists would hijack planes and fly them into significant buildings in the United States. The main target was to be the World Trade Center. The chief organizers were Osama bin Laden and a Kuwaiti named Khalid Shaikh Mohammed, who was one of the main leaders of Al-Qaeda in Afghanistan. Al-Queda was the name given to an international campaign of independent and collaborative groups that said they wanted to reduce outside influence on Islamic affairs. Bin Laden and Mohammed recruited terrorists from Afghan training camps and planned and financed the many stages of the operation.

AL-QAEDA

After the September 11 attacks, people began to talk about a worldwide terrorist organization called Al-Qaeda. The Arabic phrase "al-qaeda" means "the foundation" or "the base." It was first spoken of by radical Muslims in the late 1980s to describe the firm base they needed to support their new vision of society. It was not the name of a global terrorist network, and it was not created by Osama bin Laden. From about 1996, the term Al-Qaeda was applied to hardcore militant terrorists based in Afghanistan and Pakistan. Al-Queda has been credited with the attacks on the World Trade Center and the Pentagon and many other assaults against civilian and military targets worldwide.

49

By the summer of 2000, several of the terrorist recruits were already in the United States. The first two, Khalid al Mihdhar and Nawaf al Hazmi, had enrolled in a flying course in San Diego, California. They were slow students who were not at all interested in learning how to take off or land, but they were eager to fly jet airliners once in the air. This puzzled their instructors, who were not surprised when they left the course.

Soon afterward, three more terrorists, Mohammed Atta, Marwan al Shehhi, and Ziad Jarrah, arrived in the United States. They enrolled in flying courses in Venice, Florida. A fourth man, Hani Hanjour, was already a qualified pilot. By December 2000, all of them had gained their pilot licenses and had begun learning to operate large jet aircraft.

The next stage of the plot involved the "muscle"—the men who would back up the hijacker pilots by controlling the passengers and crew. Thirteen of them, almost all from Saudi

AHMED SHAH MASSOUD

Osama bin Laden and his colleagues had a last piece of the deadly puzzle to put in position before the September 11 attack. There was one big obstacle to the final victory of the Taliban. This was a brave and brilliant rebel leader named Ahmed Shah Massoud, who had never been defeated and who was a hero to many moderate Afghans. Many say that bin Laden needed Massoud out of the way to guarantee the Taliban's protection and cooperation in Afghanistan. On September 9, 2001, Massoud agreed to give an interview to two Arab journalists in Afghanistan. However, the journalists were in fact suicide bombers sent by Al-Qaeda. Massoud died instantly in the explosion.

Mohammed Atta was thought to be the leader of the terrorist attacks on September 11.

Arabia, came to the United States in the early summer of 2001. Slowly, they were moved from place to place, until by the end of August, they were all located near their target airports.

By the evening of September 10, everything was ready. On the East Coast of the United States, the group leader, Mohammed Atta, sent out a final message to his followers. In it, he stressed the Muslim's complete obedience to the will of Allah:

> *When you board the plane, remember that this is a battle for the sake of Allah, which is worth the whole world and all that is in it. When zero hour comes, open your chest and welcome death in the cause of Allah.*

The terrorists would take his message to heart as they prepared for their mission. Their actions would make history and create a tragedy that Americans would never forget. ◣

51

The Fall of the Twin Towers

5

Within five seconds of American Airlines Flight 11 hitting the North Tower at 8:46 A.M. on September 11, 2001, the New York Fire Department was on its way. Fire Chief Joe Pfeiffer and his crew were already out on a call to investigate a gas leak nearby. Suddenly a giant shadow came overhead with a shattering roar.

Pfeiffer watched as the airplane smashed into the World Trade Center. As fast as he could, he grabbed his telephone and called the fire station. He ordered:

Battalion 1 to Manhattan!

Then he jammed on his helmet and ran into the lobby of the North Tower. Here he set up a command post to direct operations as the fire crews arrived. Almost immediately, someone

*A passerby fell
to his knees as
the towers of the
World Trade
Center burned.*

told him that people were trapped on the 78th floor, and he sent firefighters up to deal with it. As they started up the stairs with their heavy equipment, they were passed by a stream of office workers running downward—escaping from the building.

53

These were the fortunate ones. All people above the 92nd floor were trapped because the plane had struck between the 93rd and 99th floors. The crash blocked stairwells and started a raging fire. Not one of the elevators was working. In desperation, they crowded to the windows, trying to find air to breathe away from the choking smoke. Many leaned outside the windows, and then, rather than face the blaze, jumped off to certain death hundreds of feet below. No one above the 92nd floor survived.

The fire chiefs quickly realized that their task was almost impossible. The tower had been badly damaged, and none of its electrical systems was working. Worse still, the fire was out of control. Chief Peter Hayden, who was with Pfeiffer in the lobby, later explained:

> We had a large volume of fire on the upper floors. Each floor was approximately an acre [0.4 hectares] in size.

This was far more than they could handle, so they decided that their first job was to get as many people as possible out of the building.

By this time the South Tower had been hit by United Airlines Flight 175. It crashed into the building between the 77th and 85th floors. Suddenly, the biggest disaster in New York City's history had doubled in size. Fire crews and other emergency services were still rushing to the scene and lugging out their equipment, while survivors were staggering out of the buildings.

Edmund McNally, a financial worker, spoke to his wife, Liz, from the South Tower after it was hit. She remembered his phone call:

> We said we loved each other. And we said goodbye. … It was amazing how calmly he was talking to me. Not once was he concerned about himself. I always look back on it.

By 9:50 A.M., a group of firefighters had battled their way to the 70th floor of the South Tower, where they found many dead and badly wounded people.

Nine minutes later, the South Tower collapsed. It seemed to disappear inside itself with a frightful slow-motion thunder and was gone within 10 seconds. The collapse sent ferocious clouds of dust, shattered glass, and other debris billowing out into the streets, causing terrified spectators to stampede in panic. All office workers and emergency personnel still inside the building (as well as many in the street outside) were killed in the collapse.

New Yorkers watched in horror and disbelief as the South Tower of the World Trade Center collapsed.

55

Firefighters working in the North Tower heard the roar. Within seconds, they were engulfed in a cloud of smoke and dust from the South Tower that was so thick and black that it seemed like midnight.

It was clear that if one tower was down, the other would follow soon. Immediately, the firefighters' command unit sent out a desperate order of:

> ## The Casualties
>
> In the September 11, 2001 attacks, the death toll was 2,973. This was the largest loss of life due to an enemy attack on home soil in U.S. history. The Fire Department of New York lost 343 staff members. This was the most costly disaster ever for an emergency service. The New York Police Department and the Port Authority Police Department lost 60 officers.

All units in Tower One, evacuate the building!

At 10:28 A.M., the North Tower collapsed in only 8 seconds. It was a repeat of that first nightmare roar, followed by a massive crash. Then came a black blizzard of dust and smoke that swept through the whole of downtown Manhattan. The streets were wild with panic. The police tried to organize the crowds. One officer yelled:

Come on, let's go, run on the street!

Almost everyone still inside the North Tower was killed in the collapse. Many people in neighboring buildings were crushed by falling concrete and steel.

Amazingly, a few survived. Richard "Pitch" Picciotto, a fire department battalion commander, was on the stairwell of the North Tower, several floors up, when he heard the deafening rumble

Many people saw the North Tower collapse from street level.

57

and the howl of the wind caused by the floors collapsing above him. He raced halfway down to the next level before the storm hit him, raining metal beams, chunks of concrete, and planks of timber. Then the floor gave way, and he fell into the darkness.

Injured and choked with dust, Picciotto called out to find other survivors. To his joy, several voices answered him from above and below. But they were still in great danger, as there could be further collapse. Picciotto quickly took command. He said:

> [N]obody move. This place is a house of cards.

Many people injured or overcome by the carnage of the September 11 attacks were helped to safety by colleagues or rescue workers.

The trapped men and women succeeded in making radio contact with a fire chief outside the collapsed building. They told him their location, and firefighters began the long process of digging their way in. Picciotto was trapped in the wreckage for more than four hours along with other survivors. Eventually, Picciotto led an escape by climbing up through a hole in the rubble. Using a rope and safety harness, the survivors at last met up with the rescuers and fought their way to safety.

There were two other scenes of devastation that September day. Some 200 miles (320 km) to the south of Manhattan lay the Pentagon, another symbol of American power and authority.

59

Though the scale of the disaster at the Pentagon was far less than it had been at the World Trade Center, it was still a terrible sight.

Forty-five minutes after the first attack, American Airlines Flight 77 plowed into part of the giant five-sided building. Its fuel had exploded on impact, sending blasts of fire down the corridors. Part of the western side of the building had collapsed, and 189 people had died.

Scattered across an empty Pennsylvania field about 250 miles (400 km) to the west were the fragments of United Airlines Flight 93. It had ended up near Shanksville, Pennsylvania, but the hijackers had almost certainly had another target in mind. They had probably been aiming to fly to Washington, D.C., and crash the plane into the Capitol or the White House. Most likely due to the courage of passengers who stormed the cockpit, they had gotten nowhere near these buildings.

Three days after the crash at the Pentagon, the smoke and flames had cleared. But firefighters, Federal Bureau of Investigation agents, and engineers were still working hard to clear and investigate the site.

61

At 8.55 A.M. on the morning of September 11, President George W. Bush was about to enter a second grade classroom at Emma E. Booker Elementary School in Sarasota, Florida. He was going to read and talk about education. His National Security Advisor Dr. Condoleezza Rice had just told him that an aircraft—probably a small one—had struck the World Trade Center.

Bush went into the classroom and began reading *The Pet Goat* with the children. But at 9:05, one of his aides came in and whispered:

> *A second plane hit the second tower. America is under attack.*

For a few moments, the president did not seem to react. Most likely, he was greatly stunned by the news. Then he left the school and boarded his plane, planning to return to Washington, D.C.

While in the air, President Bush called Vice President Dick Cheney. Cheney urged the president not to fly to Washington, because of the danger of further attacks. The president's jet turned west and flew to Barksdale Air Force Base in Louisiana, where it landed at about 11:45 A.M. Late that afternoon, however, Bush changed his mind and flew to Washington.

By 8:30 P.M., he was back home in the White House, where he broadcast an address to the nation. He told the American people:

> *Today, our fellow citizens, our way of life, our very freedom came under attack in a series of deliberate and deadly terrorist attacks. ... Terrorist attacks can shake the foundations of our biggest buildings, but they cannot touch the foundation of America. ... This is a day when all Americans from every walk of life unite in our resolve for justice and peace. America has stood down enemies before, and we will do so this time. None of us will ever forget this day, yet we go forward to defend freedom and all that is good and just in our world.*

President George W. Bush was visiting a school in Sarasota, Florida, when he was told of the planes hitting the World Trade Center.

As President Bush rallied a shocked and devastated nation, support for the United States began to pour in from the international community. Many countries offereed messages of sympathy and goodwill and promised to stand by the United States. Their support would soon be needed. 🔺

Preparing for War

Throughout the night of September 11, emergency service workers continued the mammoth task of searching through the ruins of the World Trade Center towers. In the days that followed, they were joined by an army of volunteer rescue workers. Many of these people drove across the United States—on their own time and using their own money—to help with the rescue and recovery work. It was a harrowing and exhausting job that would last for many months and involve more than 30,000 people.

Already journalists had named the area Ground Zero. But the firefighters and other relief workers disliked this term and never used it, because it sounded too flashy. Instead, they referred to the place as The Pile. That is what it was: a gigantic pile of crushed concrete, shattered glass, twisted steel, and a hundred other kinds of debris. All of it had to be cleared, using cranes, bulldozers, picks, and shovels.

Amid the rubble of course, was something horrible—human corpses. As they dug and lifted and hauled, the relief workers found the bodies and body parts of those killed by the first impact, by the fire, by jumping from the upper floors, or by the final collapse of the towers. Each part had to be identified and carefully removed for burial. The horror of these frequent discoveries caused enormous distress among the workers. In addition, many of the workers were working at least 80 hours a week.

Firefighters and other rescue workers worked for many weeks to sift through the wreckage of the World Trade Center.

The site was a dangerous place to work. The fires that had raged through the towers were so fierce that they were not put out for more than 100 days. This made it the longest-lasting building fire in history. The flames would suddenly flare up as a pile of papers, a piece of furniture, or some timber caught fire. The clouds of thick smoke from the ruins could be smelled miles away in Brooklyn. Many workers later suffered lung damage by inhaling the toxic dust and gases.

The fires slowed the clearance work, so a fire engine and 75 firefighters were stationed on the site every day. A constant spray of water was directed at the flames to keep them under control. One firefighter described the scene:

> *You couldn't even begin to imagine how much water was pumped in there. It was like you were creating a giant lake.*

Meanwhile, the U.S. government responded to the crisis. There were weeks of intensive meetings in Washington, D.C. Measures were taken to improve airport security and to get the country back to normal after the paralyzing nightmare of September 11. The U.S. intelligence agencies were questioned about who was responsible for the attacks. Using the information they gathered, the agencies declared that the terrorist actions had been planned and carried out by Al-Qaeda. The mastermind of the attacks had been Osama bin Laden.

On September 20, 2001, the president announced that a completely new government agency would be set up with the main job of protecting U.S. borders and preparing for any future attack. It was called the Office of Homeland Security. At the same time, the Federal Bureau of Investigation (FBI) and other law enforcement agencies began detaining all foreign nationals in the country who might possibly be connected with the attacks. More than 760 people were rounded up within a few days.

In the days following the disaster, New Yorkers posted pictures of loved ones missing in the World Trade Center attacks.

67

On September 12, 2001, George W. Bush thanked the search and rescue workers at the Pentagon crash site.

After such an attack, many wondered how the United States would deal with the rest of the world. Some in Washington, D.C., believed that the country's highest priority should be improving U.S. relations with Islamic nations and people. After all, the majority of them were eager to stay at peace. A positive and friendly approach by the United States would help to reduce the support for terrorist Muslim groups. In a speech to the nation, the president advised Americans not to make Muslims at home the target of their anger.

The president did, however, want vigorous action that would show that the United States was ready to strike back hard at any attacker. There was one obvious target for vengeance: Afghanistan. Ruled by the fundamentalist Taliban, it was the home of numerous terrorist training camps and the likely the refuge of Osama bin Laden as well as the headquarters of Al-Qaeda.

The U.S. State Department delivered a demand to the Taliban. They must hand over bin Laden and his colleagues and shut down all Al-Qaeda camps. If they did not, the United States would destroy the terrorist network in Afghanistan. These demands were delivered on September 16 by the intelligence chief of neighboring Pakistan, General Mahmoud Ahmad. The Taliban did not agree to these demands.

The State Department therefore began to prepare its battle plans for attacking the terrorists. Several other countries, including Great Britain, agreed to supply backup equipment, troops, medical assistance teams, and diplomatic support. On September 20, President Bush made another address to the nation, in which he blamed Al-Qaeda for the events of September 11. He gave a stark warning:

> *Every nation, in every region, now has a decision to make: either you are with us, or you are with the terrorists.*

The rest of the world now had a decision to make. ◣

THE WARNINGS THAT WERE IGNORED

The September 11 hijackings were not a complete surprise to the U.S. government. In May 2002, the White House acknowledged that the president had been warned of a plot by Osama bin Laden to use aircraft in an attack well before it happened. In July 2001, the Federal Aviation Administration passed on reports of "a significant threat to civil aviation." In August 2001, an Al-Qaeda suspect, Zacarias Moussaoui, was arrested at a flying school in Minnesota. (He went on trial in April 2005, and was the only person to be charged in the United States in the September 11 plot.) Also in August 2001, a Federal Bureau of Investigation agent in Arizona reported that suspected terrorists were training as pilots in the United States.

69

The Hunt for bin Laden

Chapter

7

On October 7, 2001, less than a month after the suicide hijackings, Osama bin Laden produced his own message for the people of the United States. His video was first broadcast on Al-Jazeera, the Arabic television station based in Qatar, near Saudi Arabia, in the Middle East.

The message quickly sped around the world. While he did not claim to have organized the September 11 attacks, bin Laden declared that no one in the United States would be safe while the West continued to meddle in Muslim affairs in Palestine and the Arabian Peninsula.

That same day, U.S. forces began their assault on Afghanistan. Explosives rained down on Al-Qaeda training camps and Taliban military installations, causing widespread damage. The United States retaliated against Afghanistan for the September 11 attacks, because Taliban leaders in Afghanistan did not agree to hand over Osama bin Laden. Naval vessels in the Arabian Sea fired Cruise missiles, and combat aircraft were launched from aircraft carriers. Giant B-52 bombers thundered through the skies from their long-range bases in the Indian Ocean.

By mid-October, U.S. ground troops were moving in to attack key sites and set up command centers in Afghanistan.

BIN LADEN'S BROADCAST

In his October 7, 2001 videotape, Osama bin Laden said:

Here is the United States. It was filled with terror from its north to its south and from its east to its west. What the United States tastes today is a very small thing compared to what we have tasted for tens of years. Our nation has been tasting this humiliation and contempt for more than 80 years. ... I swear by Almighty God that neither the United States nor he who lives in the United States will enjoy security before we can see it as a reality in Palestine and before all the infidel armies leave the land of Mohammed.

Osama bin Laden spoke to U.S. leaders and citizens in a videotape that was broadcast in October 2001. He said that God had struck against the United States and destroyed its two greatest buildings.

The Taliban had no answer to the overwhelming firepower and efficiency of the invading forces. They were also faced with an army of Afghans—the Northern Alliance, which had always fought against their domination. Together, U.S. and Northern Alliance soldiers captured the key town of Mazar-e-Sharif.

The Taliban was now in full flight across much of Afghanistan. On November 13, its members fled

These soldiers helped to secure Bagram Airbase, located about 27 miles (47 km) north of Kabul, Afghanistan. The airbase was a vital target for U.S. troops invading Afghanistan.

from Afghanistan's capital, Kabul, and by the end of the month, all major cities were in the hands of the United States and its allies. On December 22, a new government took over, led by Hamid Karzai, who was from the southern part of Afghanistan. The operation seemed to have been a huge success.

But where was Osama bin Laden? He had not been seen since November 14. At the very beginning of the invasion, U.S. Special Forces agents had secretly landed in Afghanistan with orders to bring him out, dead or alive. Since then, growing numbers of troops had been scouring the White Mountains, very near the border of Pakistan. Bin Laden was known to have a hideout there, in the caves at Tora Bora.

Tora Bora

The Tora Bora area is riddled with limestone caves, formed where streams have enlarged the natural cracks in the rock. During the Soviet occupation of the 1980s, many Afghan resistance fighters had hidden in them. Osama bin Laden used a large part of his fortune to dig out and equip these caves as a military stronghold, complete with storerooms, ventilator shafts, heating, and a water supply. Some may even have been big enough to conceal trucks and armored vehicles.

After the retreat of the Taliban, thousands of fundamentalist fighters had fled into the mountains of the south. Many experts believed that the United States had not sent enough soldiers to block their escape routes. One Afghan politician said:

> *The U.S. operation was like Swiss cheese, with too many big holes.*

73

Afghan fighters hostile to the Taliban watched as U.S. aircraft bombed the Tora Bora caves in the mountains, thought to be the refuge of Osama bin Laden.

The result was that most of the militants vanished across the border to Iran or to Pakistan. Osama bin Laden and several other important terrorist leaders may well have been among them.

U.S. forces and their allies had advanced to the Tora Bora cave system by late November and begun a massive bombardment of rockets, bombs, and shells on all likely entrances. The battle lasted 18 days, and then Afghan, American, and British soldiers climbed up for the final attack on the complex. They found nobody inside except for a few ragged and wounded Taliban. There was no sign of bin Laden.

Over the course of the fighting in Afghanistan, the U.S. military had taken large numbers of prisoners. Many of these were detained because they were suspected of having links with Al-Qaeda and other terrorist organizations. In January 2002, the Americans began flying these men to a brand new prison camp built specially for them on the far side of the Atlantic Ocean. It was inside the U.S. naval base at Guantanamo Bay in Cuba.

As the base was not located on U.S. soil, it was unclear whether prisoners there had legal rights under the U.S. Constitution. They could be kept there indefinitely without a trial. The conditions at Guantanamo Bay soon drew protests from humanitarian groups all over the world. ◣

GUANTANAMO BAY

Human rights organizations voiced serious concerns about the use of Guantanamo Bay for a military prison. U.S. officials at Guantanamo Bay were criticized when photographs taken in 2003 were published showing prison guards torturing inmates. In 2005, guards also reportedly damaged inmates' copies of the Koran, a sacred book for Muslims.

The World After September 11

On January 29, 2002, President George W. Bush gave his yearly State of the Union address in Washington, D.C. He said:

We are winning our war on terror.

However, Bush warned that this war was only in its early stages. He went on to condemn three specific countries—North Korea, Iran, and Iraq. These states, he said, encouraged acts of terror and aggression against the United States and the West. Bush said:

[These countries] constitute an axis of evil, aiming to threaten the peace of the world.

The president seemed to be preparing the way for more aggressive American action against foreign nations in the future. His message was that the war on terrorism was simply a struggle of good against evil, but Al-Qaeda saw its war against the United States in the same terms.

On January 29, 2002, President Bush made his State of the Union address to a joint session of Congress.

IN GOD WE TRUST

On March 11, 2002, two memorial services were held at Ground Zero in New York City, to mark the six-month anniversary of the event. Work stopped on the site for almost the first time since September. One ceremony was held at 8:46 A.M. Another was held that night. After a two-minute silence, two powerful lights were switched on at the site. They sent beams high into the sky to symbolize the twin towers.

On May 30, the last steel beam standing on the site of the World Trade Center was hauled away. The gigantic cleanup operation was finally over. It had been completed faster and had cost less than expected. Originally, cleanup costs were estimated at several billion dollars. They actually were closer to about $750 million. A big question after the cleanup was completed was how the area should be rebuilt.

The site would always be a grave for many of the September 11 victims, and so it should include a memorial to them. But it was also a prime piece of real estate in the business and financial heart of New York City. Rebuilding there would also make a statement that the American spirit could not be defeated. The government promised cash rewards for companies who agreed to stay on the site, though many decided to leave for other parts of Manhattan. Even the New York Stock Exchange threatened to move out to New Jersey, but it ended up staying in Manhattan.

The first anniversary of September 11 was marked in countries all around the world. In the

United States itself, mourners gathered at Ground Zero early in the morning. A New York Police Department helicopter could be seen protectively circling the Statue of Liberty. Firefighters and construction workers filed into the huge empty space.

By March 2002, more than 1.4 million tons of debris had been cleared from the World Trade Center site.

79

At 8:46 A.M. exactly, the memorial service began. Rudy Giuliani, who had been New York's mayor in 2001, began to read out the names of all the people who had been killed, in alphabetical order. As the morning wore on, others took over from him—relatives, politicians, film stars, and schoolchildren. Meanwhile, President Bush visited all three of the crash sites, attending ceremonies in New York, at the Pentagon, and on the field in Shanksville, Pennslyvania.

Bush was still determined to push ahead with the war on terror. He was spurred on by fresh atrocities. Soon after the anniversary of September 11, three bombs exploded on the Indonesian island of Bali, killing 202 people. The attack was carried out by Muslim terrorists, but it had no connection with Osama bin Laden himself or with Al-Qaeda. All the same, it encouraged the U.S. administration to prepare for military action against at least one member of the "axis of evil."

People from all over the world came to New York on September 11, 2002, to attend a memorial ceremony making the first anniversary of the tragedy.

Enemy number two (after Afghanistan) was Iraq. Long before September 11, several of Bush's closest advisers had been convinced that Saddam Hussein, Iraq's leader, had been aiding and sheltering Al-Qaeda plotters. On the day after the hijackings, the president had ordered one of his security aides to try to find a connection between Iraq and Al-Qaeda. Now, a year later, he was pressing hard for war in Iraq.

Many people in other countries disagreed with President Bush. They pointed out that there was no obvious link between Iraq and Osama bin Laden or the September 11 attacks. However, Bush was also convinced that Iraq had weapons of mass

destruction (WMDs), such as nuclear missiles and poison gases. Inspectors from the United Nations spent many months in Iraq searching for these but found none.

Eventually the president decided that he could wait no longer. Despite protests from the United Nations, he ordered an invasion of Iraq that started on March 20, 2003. His main allies were Great Britain and Australia, but about 24 other countries provided military support. In an operation using what were called "shock and awe" tactics, U.S. forces began a thunderous air strike on Baghdad, the capital city of Iraq. The next day ground troops swept into the country.

Hundreds of U.S. tanks and other armored vehicles took part in the push to gain control of Baghdad at the climax of the invasion of Iraq in April 2003.

83

The invasion itself brought swift and overwhelming victory for the United States and its allies. By mid-April, Saddam's government had collapsed and his army had been disbanded. However, the conquerors have been unable to gain complete control over the country, and more than 2,000 coalition soldiers have died. No evidence of WMDs has ever been found, even after careful searching. Though a dangerous dictator had been removed from power, no link between Iraq and the events of September 11 has been discovered.

On top of all this, as of November 2005, Osama bin Laden had not been caught. Some believed he was dead, but in October 2004 he appeared on a new video that was broadcast by the Al-Jazeera TV network. He addressed the American people directly:

> *I am amazed at you. Although almost four years have passed since the [September 11] incidents, Bush is still practicing distortion and confusion. Your security is in your own hands. Each state that does not tamper with our security will have assured its own security.*

The dreadful events of September 11, 2001, have left a deep scar on the collective American soul. Aside from the massive loss of life, many Americans were appalled that their national security was so easily breached by a handful of terrorists.

The United States today is a more wary country,

with less trust in the intentions of foreign powers, whether they are friendly or not. At the same time, the tragedy has served as a common experience, one which has played a part in uniting Americans and helping them understand one another a little better. ◤

On the first anniversary of the attacks, pilots and flight attendants shared their grief at the UA Flight 93 crash site near Shanksville, Pennsylvania.

85

Timeline

1979

Islamist revolution in Iran overthrows the shah; American hostages are seized in Tehran; Soviet troops invade Afghanistan

1984

 Osama bin Laden and other militant leaders establish training camps

1989

Soviet troops withdraw from Afghanistan; a sustained revolt in Algeria by an Islamist group leads to a long period of brutal repression

February 26, 1993

A car bomb explodes under the World Trade Center

1995

Islamist terrorists attempt to kill Egypt's president; a bomb destroys the Egyptian Embassy in Islamabad

1996

The Taliban seize Kabul and become rulers of Afghanistan; the Taliban fail to defeat the Northern Alliance, led by Ahmed Shah Massoud

1997

Terrorists murder 58 European tourists in Luxor, Egypt

1998

Osama bin Laden announces the formation of the World Islamic Front and declares war on the United States and its allies; car bombs explode at U.S. embassies in Nairobi and Dar-es-Salaam; the United States hits back with air strikes against Sudan and Afghanistan

October 2000

 Boat packed with explosives damages USS *Cole* near Aden harbor; first members of September 11 terrorist group have arrived in the United States to begin pilot training

September 9, 2001

Ahmed Shah Masood assassinated by Muslim extremists in Afghanistan

September 11, 2001

7:30 A.M.

Five terrorists board American Airlines (AA) Flight 11 at Logan Airport in Boston

7:40 A.M.

Five terrorists board United Airlines (UA) Flight 175 at Logan Airport in Boston

7:48 A.M.

Four terrorists board UA Flight 93 at Newark Airport in New Jersey

7:50 A.M.

Five terrorists board AA Flight 77, at Dulles Airport, near Washington, D.C.

7:59 A.M.

AA Flight 11 takes off from Boston

8:14 A.M.

Hijacking of AA Flight 11 begins; UA Flight 175 takes off from Boston

8:20 A.M.

AA Flight 77 takes off from near Washington, D.C.

8:42 A.M.

Hijacking of UA Flight 175 begins; UA Flight 93 takes off from Newark

8:46 A.M.

AA Flight 11 hits the North Tower of the World Trade Center

8:51 A.M.

Hijacking of AA Flight 77 begins

9:03 A.M.

UA Flight 175 hits the South Tower of the World Trade Center

9:05 A.M.

President Bush given news of attacks

9:37 A.M.

AA Flight 77 crashes into the Pentagon

9:45 A.M.

The White House and the Capitol building are evacuated

9:59 A.M.

The South Tower of the World Trade Center collapses

10:02 A.M.

UA Flight 93 crashes into an open field at Shanksville, Pennsylvania, after passengers counterattack

10:28 A.M.

North Tower of the World Trade Center collapses

September 16, 2001

The United States demands that the Taliban give up Osama bin Laden and his colleagues

October 2001

Homeland Security Council established in the United States; the United States launches air strikes on Afghanistan, followed by a land invasion

Timeline

November 2001

The Taliban abandon Kabul; the invaders bombard and search the Tora Bora caves, but they do not capture Osama bin Laden

December 2001

A new government is established in Afghanistan after the fall of the Taliban

January 2002

Al-Qaeda suspects taken to prison camp at Guantanamo Bay, Cuba; George W. Bush gives speech referring to "axis of evil"

March 11, 2002

A memorial service for victims of September 11 attacks is held at Ground Zero

May 30, 2002

The clearance of World Trade Center site is completed

September 11, 2002

 Ceremonies are held to mark the first anniversary of September 11 at all three crash sites

October 2002

A terrorist attack kills 202 in Bali

March 2003

United States undertakes air strikes on Iraq that are followed by a land invasion

October 2004

Osama bin Laden addresses American people in a videotape broadcast on the Al-Jazeera television network

November 2004

George W. Bush re-elected as president

September 2005

The death toll among coalition troops in Iraq reaches more than 2,080

September 11, 2005

Ceremonies are held to mark the fourth anniversary of September 11 at all three crash sites

ON THE WEB

For more information on this topic, use FactHound.

1 Go to *www.facthound.com*

2 Type in this book ID: 075651620X

3 Click on the *Fetch It* button.

FactHound will find the best Web sites for you.

HISTORIC SITES

The Pentagon
Alexandria, VA 22301
703/697-1776
Tours of the Pentagon, the headquarters of the U.S.
Department of Defense, are available by reservation only.

Shanksville Memorial Site
Skyline Drive
Shanksville, PA

National Park Service
109 West Main St.
Suite 104
Somerset, PA 15501-2035
814/443-4557
Visitors can view a temporary memorial near the spot where
United Airlines Flight 93 crashed.

World Trade Center site ("Ground Zero")
Church Street (between Liberty and Vesey streets)
New York, NY
Visitors can view the site where the World Trade Center towers
once stood and see current construction projects.

Glossary

Allah

the supreme being, or one God, of the Muslim religion

battalion

a unit of personnel in the armed forces or emergency forces

communist

country or person practicing communism, a political system in which there is no private property and everything is owned and shared in common

extremist

a person who puts forward extreme or violent ideas and commits acts to support them

fanatical

driven by excessive enthusiasm and uncritical devotion

foreign national

in the United States, any person other than a U.S. citizen, a U.S. legal resident alien, or a person in U.S. custody

fundamentalist

a person who believes unquestioningly in a set of basic and unalterable religious ideas

hijack

to take control of an aircraft or other vehicle by force

hostage

a person taken by force and held as a way of securing an agreement; a hostage's life is often threatened in order to persuade one's enemies to give in to a demand

infidel

a person who has no faith in any religion; This term has been used to describe those who do not believe in the Islamic faith

militant

a person who is aggressive or warlike in pursuing some cause or ideal

missile

a weapon that is fired at, thrown at, or dropped on a target

mosque

a Muslim house of worship

petroleum

the raw material for fuel oil that is found under the ground and processed into a variety of chemicals including gasoline, kerosene, and natural gas

terrorism

the use of violence and intimidation to make other people afraid and to achieve a political or religious goal

truss

a part of a wooden or metal framework, used to support walls or a roof

SOURCE NOTES

Chapter 1

Page 11, line 21: National Commission on Terrorist Attacks. *The 9/11 Commission Report.* New York: W.W. Norton, 2004, p. 6.

Page 14, sidebar: "United in Courage."
<http://www.whatreallyhappened.com/people.html>

Page 14, line 14: Ibid., p. 7.

Page 14, line 21: Ibid., p. 8.

Page 18, line 15: National Commission on Terrorist Attacks. *The 9/11 Commission Report.* New York: W.W. Norton, 2004, p. 11.

Page 18, line 23: "September 11 Report." *The Observer.* 2 Dec. 2001.

Page 18, line 26: Ibid.

Page 19, line 7: Ibid.

Page 21, line 2: National Commission on Terrorist Attacks. *The 9/11 Commission Report.* New York: W.W. Norton, 2004, p. 14.

Chapter 2

Page 31, line 3: Sayyid Qutb. *Milestones.* Burr Ridge, Illinois: American Trust Publications, 1990, p. 51.

Page 31, line 17: Ibid.

Chapter 3

Page 36, line 4: Jason Burke. *Al-Qaeda: The True Story of Radical Islam.* New York: I.B. Tauris, 2004, p. 73.

Page 37, sidebar: Malise Ruthven. *A Fury for God.* New York: Granta, 2002, p.79.

Chapter 4

Page 44, line 18: Jason Burke. *Al-Qaeda: The True Story of Radical Islam.* New York: I.B. Tauris, 2004, p. 175.

Page 51, line 10: Ibid., p. 253.

Chapter 5

Page 52, line 12: Dennis Smith. *Report from Ground Zero.* New York: Doubleday, 2002, p. 24.

Page 54, line 18: Ibid., p. 37.

Page 55, line 15: James Glanz. "Accounts From the South Tower."
<http://www.nytimes.com>

Source Notes

Page 56, line 16: Dennis Smith. *Report from Ground Zero.* New York: Doubleday, 2002, p. 55.

Page 56, line 24: "Attack on America." *The Guardian Unlimited.* 2001.

Page 58, line 13: Richard Picciotto. *Last Man Down.* New York: Berkeley Books, 2002, p. 118.

Page 62, line 13: National Commission on Terrorist Attacks. *The 9/11 Commission Report.* New York: W.W. Norton, 2004, p. 38.

Page 63, line 1: "The President's Address to the Nation." 11 Sept. 2001. CNN.com <http://www.cnn.com/2001/US/09/11/bush.speech.text/>

Chapter 6
Page 66, line 16: Dennis Smith. *Report from Ground Zero.* New York: Doubleday, 2002, p. 249.

Page 69, line 27: White House News Archive. <http://www.whitehouse.gov/news/releases/2001/09>

Chapter 7
Page 71, sidebar: "Bin Laden: America 'Filled With Fear.'" <http://archives.cnn.com/2001/WORLD/asiapcf/central/10/07/ret.binladen.transcript/>

Page 73, line 29: Jason Burke. *Al-Qaeda: The True Story of Radical Islam.* New York: I.B. Tauris, 2004, p. 266.

Chapter 8
Page 76, line 4: White House News Archive. <http://www.whitehouse.gov/news/releases/2002/01>

Page 76, line 11: Ibid.

Page 84, line 19: BBC News Online. <http://news.bbc.co.uk/2/hi/middle_east/3966817.stm>

Select Bibliography

Burke, Jason. *Al-Qaeda: The True Story of Radical Islam.* New York: I.B. Tauris, 2004.

Clarke, Richard A. *Against All Enemies: Inside America's War on Terror.* New York: Free Press, 2004.

Mueller, Lavonne. *Voices From September 11th.* New York: Applause, 2002.

Murphy, Dean. *September 11: An Oral History.* New York: Doubleday, 2002.

National Commission on Terrorist Attacks. *The 9/11 Commission Report.* New York: W.W. Norton, 2004.

Picciotto, Richard. *Last Man Down.* New York: Berkeley Books, 2002.

Ruthven, Malise. *A Fury for God.* New York: Granta, 2002.

Thoms, Annie, ed. *With Their Eyes: September 11th—The View from a High School at Ground Zero.* New York: Harper Tempest, 2002.

Smith, Dennis. *Report from Ground Zero.* New York: Doubleday, 2002.

Further Reading

Frank, Mitch. *Understanding September 11th: Answering Questions About the Attacks on America.* New York: Viking Books, 2002.

Harwayne, Shelley. *Messages to Ground Zero: Children Respond To September 11, 2001.* Chicago: Heinemann Library, 2002.

Macdonald, Fiona. *The September 11th Terrorist Attacks: Days That Changed The World.* New York: World Almanac Library, 2004.

Index

ABOUT THE AUTHOR

Andrew Langley is the author of many history books for children. These include a biography of Mikhail Gorbachev, *The Roman News,* and *A Castle at War,* which was shortlisted for the Times Education Supplement Information Book Award.

IMAGE CREDITS